GOLDEN GIFTS

LEGACY STUDY ACTIVITY BOOK

A Tree is as Strong As Its Roots

By *Melvia F. Miller*

GOLDEN GIFTS

LEGACY STUDY ACTIVITY BOOK

Published by **Edutainment Enterprises**

Printed in the U.S.A.

This book belongs to: _____

Phone = ___(_____)_____

DEDICATION:

This book is dedicated to my 2 wonderful sons, Malik and Mikal, who have been the light and delight of my life. My sons are very special people and will receive most of the benefits, proceeds and honors derived from the sales of my books. I could not have accomplished the completion of this book without my 2 sons.

THANKS:

A SPECIAL THANKS TO MY MOTHER AND FATHER for raising me. I could not have accomplished this writing project without the help, support and love of all of my many friends. I deeply appreciate all of the people who have assisted me in various ways throughout my life.

~Melvia F. Miller *(aka: "the Soulful Dr. Seuss)*

We donate a portion of our profits and some books to youth groups, schools and other good causes.

WORDS OF WISDOM

"A climate of alienation has a profound effect upon the Black personality. Often the effect is so crushing that some Black people who have evidence of the truth, still find it hard to accept the fact that (Negroes) Blacks really were the first to civilize the world."

~Quote from **Cheikh Anta Diop** (historian and author)

"There is no Negro problem. The problem is whether the American people have loyalty enough, honor enough, patriotism enough, to live up to their own constitution."
~Frederick Douglass (abolitionist & publisher)

"For Africa to me... is more than a glamorous fact. It is a historical truth. No man can know where he is going unless he knows exactly where he has been and exactly how he arrived at his present place."
~ Dr. Maya Angelou (poetess)

"Black people have always been America's wilderness in search of a promised land."
~Cornel West, *"Nihilism in America,"* Race Matters, 1993

"For I am my mother's daughter, and the drums of Africa still beat in my heart."
~Mary McLeod Bethune

TABLE OF CONTENTS

HOW MUCH DO YOU KNOW ABOUT THESE EVENTS AND INCIDENTS IN HISTORY? WHAT DO YOU KNOW ABOUT LEADERS, HEROES AND ACHIEVERS?

A NOTE FROM THE AUTHOR

This activity book is designed so that readers can participate in documenting various issues and events and thus SPICING UP the study of history – via expressing creative ideas. This way of studying can be a cathartic *(emotional release, tension relieving, illuminating)* tool...in a way similar to how therapists and counselors suggest using journaling.

> For as long as people have lived, they have written things down. On the walls of temples, structures, and caves, on parchment paper, on scrolls, on signs, in books, and inventing machines that permitting other ways of writing down information. Mankind's desire to write is as old as his ideas, and it has been used as a form of communication for centuries. Possibly one of the most potent forms of education is a person communicating to and with oneself, and to the world, in the form of a diary or journal. Writing down your ideas help to open your mind to explore new ways of viewing something. Participating in creative projects enhances the opportunity for brilliance to emerge from those who are doing the project.

Using pictures, along with historical facts and information makes learning history fun. A picture is worth a thousand words, but a few words added to the picture complete the story.

* * *

> *"If you want to understand your present*
> *circumstances, review your past actions.*
> *If you want to know your future circumstances,*
> *...examine your present actions."*
>
> ~ ancient Mongolian Proverb

ANCESTORS LEFT US GOLDEN GIFTS OF WISDOM, INVENTIONS, MEDICINES, AND OTHER GIFTS.

INTRODUCTION

HOW MUCH DO YOU KNOW ???

Imagine walking down the street on a hot summer day in a new pair of shoes, having left the Beauty Shop where you left your African-American girlfriend who was getting her hair done. Then you stop on the corner at the traffic light to wait for the green light. Several big semi-trucks stop on a dime because they have the red traffic signal light.

As you stand there you notice some children eating ice cream and their mother is talking on her cell phone. You had left the shop to just take a walk to see the sights of the city, but you need to find a bathroom first. You go into one of the office buildings and use the toilet. You get on an elevator and ride up to the third floor. While you are in that building, you enjoy the cool air from the air conditioner...and you stop to sharpen your pencil so that you can finish writing a letter that you started earlier... as soon as you find a calm place to sit.

Then you start back out on your walk again...and this time you notice a small jazz band playing in the park. So--before sitting down, you go into the near-by *"Health Food Store"* and purchase an herbal health drink."--Then you walk over to the park and sit down and listen to the soothing jazz for a while and sip on your herbal drink. After writing your letter -- you decide to read a book concerning predictions of *"modern-time Earth calamities"* -- made by ancient wise people thousands of years ago.

Question: WHAT DO ALL OF THESE SITUATIONS AND PRODUCTS HAVE IN COMMON ?

*BRIEF BACKGROUND ON AFRICA ...
A VERY SIGNIFICANT PLACE IN THE HISTORY OF ALL HUMANITY !

DID YOU KNOW..?

AFRICA is known as the "motherland" and the "cradle of civilization."

The oldest human artifacts and bones have been found in Africa.

Scholars have discovered that medicines and many great inventions of all types, including: airplanes and electric batteries -- were first created in Africa.

Many ancient scholars -- such as PLATO studied in schools in ancient Africa.

A combination of various tribes of Negroid people: Nubians, Kushites, and West Africans engaged in mutual trade and commerce along the coasts of West Africa could have planned many trips to and from the Americas and could have conducted a crossing about 1200 B.C. and afterwards.

European explorers were <u>not</u> the first to find the Americas. When Columbus landed in the Americas -- Black Indians met him. Africans had been to the Americas and traded with the so-called Indians long before the Europeans thought of it. In fact, at one time in history, Africa was the *"New York"* of the world, where all new inventions, products, and concepts were found.

Black people had their own civilizations, schools, temples, sciences, and many so-called modern conveniences hundreds of years before 1492 when Christopher Columbus sailed to the Americas.

*****

"The African-American experience is one of the most important threads in the American tapestry."
~ Bill Frist (U.S. Senator)

Nubia *(Land of Gold):* The *Kingdom of Kush (also called Nubia)* was located on the Nile River, to the south of ancient Egypt. Archaeologists have found material evidence of several early cultures in Nubian beginning about 3500 B.C. Unlike Egypt, they were not dependent upon the flooding of the Nile for good soil. They enjoyed tropical rainfall all year long.

The earliest inhabitants of what is now *The Sudan* can be traced back to the most ancient dark-skinned races of African (i.e., Negroid) peoples who lived in the vicinity of Khartoum, the Sudan, in Mesolithic (Middle Stone Age) times (30,000-20,000 BC). The Kush Kingdom had iron and gold. Trade was very important to Kush. They established flourishing ports on the Red Sea. They had trade agreements with nearby Egypt that would allow them free access to the Mediterranean via the Nile River. Egyptians depended on Kush for iron, gold, and for exotic goods like incense and ebony.

SPIRITUAL PRACTICES: The sun was often recognized as a giver of life and even within pagan religions where many gods were worshipped, the sun god was often given a high status. To many civilizations that worshipped the sun, it comes as no surprise that gold was seen as a valuable representation of the sun, given its shinny yellow attributes. Gold was considered the 'skin of the gods.' Gold, silver and other metals were also used in 'religious' ceremonies and believed to help one to ascend to higher dimensions.

The **Great Pyramid of Giza** (called the **Pyramid of Khufu** and the **Pyramid of Cheops**) is the oldest and largest of the three pyramids in the Giza Necropolis bordering what is now El Giza, Egypt. It is the oldest of the Seven Wonders of the Ancient World, and the only one to remain largely intact. The Great Pyramid consists of an estimated 2.3 million limestone blocks with most believed to have been transported from nearby quarries.   There are many theories as to how the pyramids were built – but one fact is for sure – the builders had highly advanced knowledge of architecture, construction, and related issues. Even modern builders cannot fully explain how it was done.

Ancient Nubia is one of the richest areas of Egypt in terms of ancient monuments. Nubia contains 16 temples. Questions remain in many scholarly circles as to who the giant statues (in Egyptian temples) represent ....located in Abu Simbelin, **Nubia**, southern Egypt. The statues are sculptural masterpieces. The twin temples were originally carved out of the mountainside. These amazing structures were discovered by western explorers in 1813.

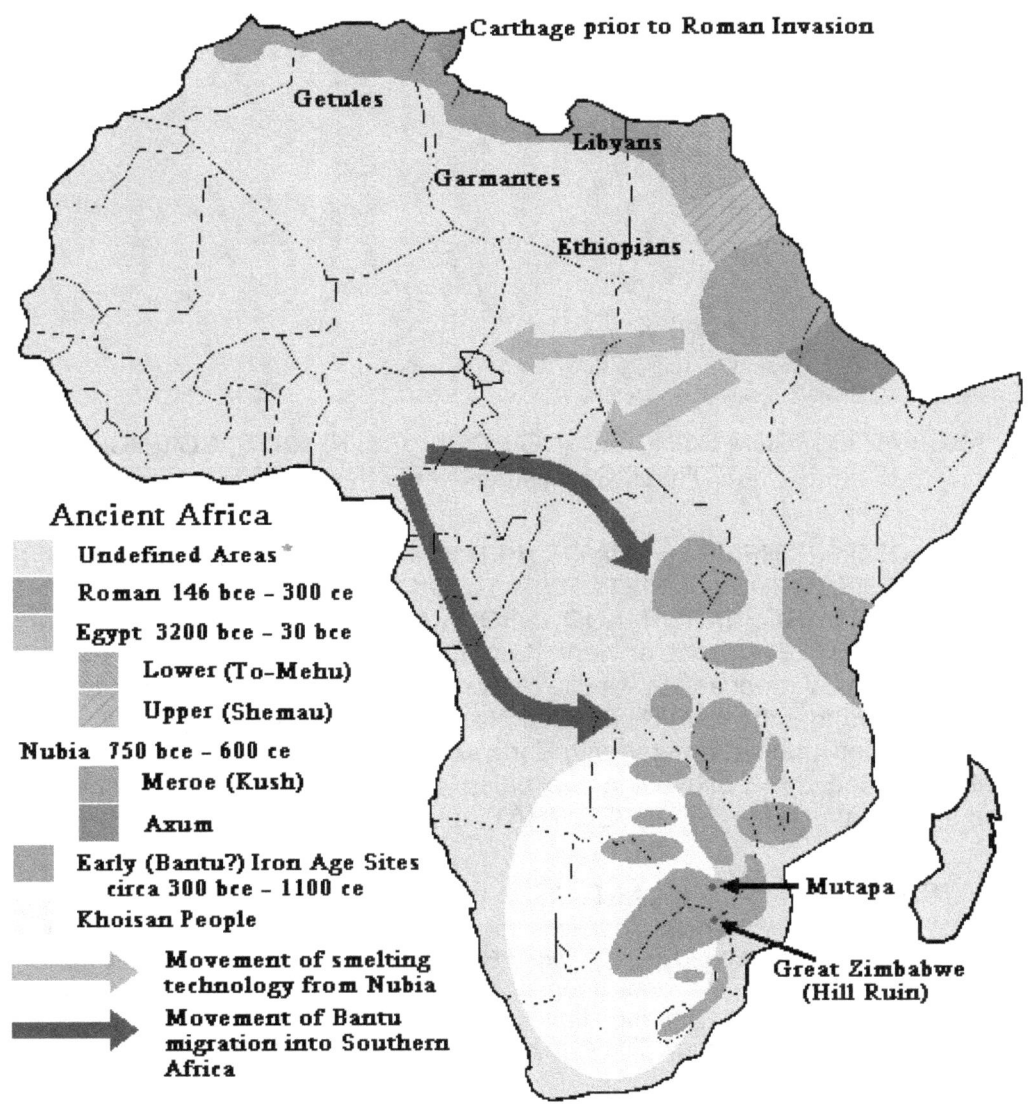

Carthage prior to Roman Invasion

Getules

Libyans

Garmantes

Ethiopians

Ancient Africa

Undefined Areas *

Roman 146 bce – 300 ce

Egypt 3200 bce – 30 bce

    Lower (To-Mehu)

    Upper (Shemau)

Nubia 750 bce – 600 ce

    Meroe (Kush)

    Axum

Early (Bantu?) Iron Age Sites
circa 300 bce – 1100 ce

Khoisan People

Movement of smelting
technology from Nubia

Movement of Bantu
migration into Southern
Africa

Mutapa

Great Zimbabwe
(Hill Ruin)

ANCIENT WISDOM CONCERNING ECOLOGY, PLANTS, SCIENCES, AND
ASTROLOGY ORIGINATED IN AFRICA

THE ONE THEME THAT PERMEATES THE OLDEST WRITINGS, ANCIENT RECORDS, HISTORY BOOKS, RELIGIOUS ARTIFACTS, DOCUMENTS, RESEARCH AND INFORMATION OBTAINED REGARDING THE ANCIENT PEOPLE - -from ancient Kemet...to the old Chinese Dynasty...to the Olmecs in the Americas...to Native American Indians in No. America --- is that they believed that the EARTH (Mother Nature; Gaia) was a living being -- and that survival relied upon harmony with Earth's elements. They studied the stars and planets.... and they believed in the union and connect-ness of nature, science and spirituality. THEY BELIEVED THAT ALL IS CONNECTED... *(a holistic view)*.

SECRETS OF THE PYRAMIDS.... What purpose did these massive structures serve? Why were they scattered across the desert in a seemingly random pattern? The pyramid mystery deepened in 1993 when Rudolf Gantenbrink discovered a secret door in the Great Pyramid -- a door unopened for 4,500 years. Robert Bauval and Adrian Gilbert have uncovered for the first time the key to the plan that governed the construction of the pyramids. The evidence points to highly advanced technology.

Although most Americans think that the (Caucasian) FOUNDING FATHERS of the U.S. (Jefferson, Washington, Benjamin Franklin, etc.) created the concepts of **'democracy'** -- that is not entirely accurate. Those ideas originated a long time ago....among the ancient Africans.

Part One

AFRICA

phillipmartin.com

"....A tree that develops a deep, <u>strong</u> root structure can withstand heavy winds without toppling to the ground."

THIS WORKBOOK WILL RENDER BEST RESULTS WHEN USED IN CONJUNCTION WITH OTHER ACTIVITIES, SUCH AS -- SEMINARS, WATCHING FILMS, ACADEMIC GAMES, AND GROUP EXERCISES.

PARTICIPANTS CAN ALSO USE THIS WORKBOOK FOR THEIR OWN SELF-HELP. USERS SHOULD WRITE IN WHAT THEY LEARNED....FACTS, DATA, PLACES, CONCEPTS, AND THEIR OWN REACTIONS, RESPONSES, AND INFO.... IN THE BLANKS PROVIDED ... OR USE EXTRA SHEETS, IF NEEDED.

Africa is not a country. It is a continent like Asia or So. America -- so it must be realized that it has as many various styles as in our Western continents too. The *"Motherland"* has been home to many advanced, mystical and exotic civilizations. Many have been buried beneath the sands of time, but others are known.

WHAT DO YOU KNOW ABOUT AFRICA? _____

_____

_____

WHAT DO YOU KNOW ABOUT EACH OF THESE ANCIENT TREASURES ?

Nubia is considered to be the first human civilization to survive for a long time period. How were they different from Egypt?   Why was GOLD so important to them?

WRITE DOWN A FEW FACTS ABOUT WHAT IS IN THIS PICTURE AND DESCRIBE WHAT YOU LEARN FROM IT --

_____

_____

_____

HOW HAVE/COULD THESE **GIFTS** HELP MODERN SOCIETY—

_____

_____

Ma'at was personified as a <u>goddess</u> and was the <u>Ancient Egyptian</u> concept of <u>truth</u>, balance, order, <u>law</u>, <u>morality</u>, and <u>justice</u>. The original *Emerald Tablet* dates back prior to 30,000 BC. The main purpose of the *Emerald Tablet* was that it is a record of significant historical events…and it also contained a great deal of high-level spiritual wisdom.

WRITE DOWN A FEW FACTS ABOUT WHAT IS IN THESE
PICTURES AND DESCRIBE WHAT YOU LEARN FROM IT --

_____

_____

_____

HOW HAVE/COULD THESE **GIFTS** HELP MODERN SOCIETY--

_____

_____

WRITE A SHORT PARAGRAPH ABOUT THE **PAST HISTORY**
A TIME WHEN THESE CULTURES FLOURISHED IN THEIR OWN
GOLDEN ERA --- FOR EACH OF THESE PLACES …
(*For example, give:* dates, location, arts, foods, religion, etc.)

Alkebulan = _____

_____

Atlantis = _____

_____

Kemet = _____

_____

Nubia = _____

_____

Timbuktu = _____

_____

NOTE: Use another sheet of paper if you wish to write more….or make a scrap-book

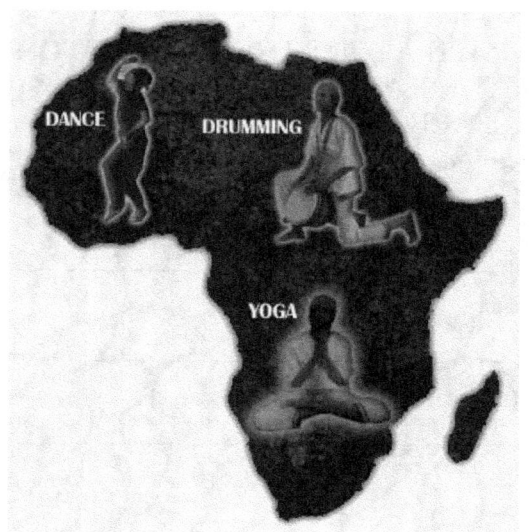 

WRITE DOWN A FEW FACTS ABOUT WHAT IS IN THESE PICTURES AND DESCRIBE WHAT YOU LEARN FROM IT --

_____

_____

_____

_____

HOW HAVE/COULD THESE **GIFTS** HELP MODERN SOCIETY--

_____

_____

IN PHOTO: Royal **Kente cloth** being hand woven in a loom.

WRITE DOWN A FEW FACTS ABOUT WHAT IS IN THESE PICTURES AND
DESCRIBE WHAT YOU LEARN FROM IT --

_____

_____

_____

HOW HAVE/COULD THESE **GIFTS** HELP MODERN SOCIETY--

_____

_____

_____

IN PHOTO -- Mud cloth hanging outside.

"Mud cloth" is a long established tradition among the people in Mali. The origin of this cloth is believed to lie in central Mali. Mud-cloth is a living art form, with techniques and motifs passed down from generations of mothers to daughters. Hand woven and hand-dyed mud-cloth uses a centuries old process using numerous applications of various plant juices/teas and mud to dye hand woven cotton cloth.

LIST A FEW MORE FACTS ABOUT THIS AFRICAN FABRIC:

1) _____

2) _____

3) _____

How much do you know about the history of African women and how they have been treated?

Write in where they ruled with dates of these following listed ancient African queens –

Queen Makeda _____

Queen Candace _____

Queen Nefertiti _____

*CAN YOU LIST OTHER ANCIENT **AFRICAN QUEENS** and their achievements ?

The Fountain of Youth

For thousands of years, people have searched for ways to stay young , healthy, and to avoid sickness. Men have dreamed of being able to live forever. Back in the 1400's an explorer named **Ponce de Leon** followed in the footsteps of **Christopher Columbus** --- searching for a mythical **'fountain of youth"** in the area that Europeans called 'the New World.' It was rumored that there was a fountain or pond of water in the area now called Bimini (in the Bahamas) which contained special "life-giving" waters.

The ancient *'medicine men'* of Kemet (Egypt) used many forms of plants, fruit juices, herbal medicines, water, psycho-therapy treatments, and other botanical remedies -- even surgery long ago.

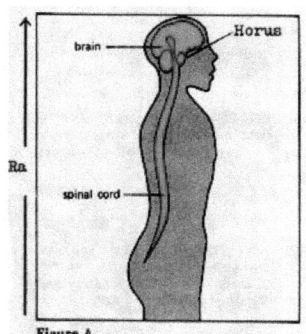

The glands and hornones clean up the spinal colunn to raise up the Ra-consciousness which opens the third-eye of Horus. This is achieved through the proper nutrition of grains, minerals, vitamins, and trace elements which produces healthy tissue in the body. This ancient Egyptian concept is alluded to in Matthew ch. 6: 19-27 of the Holy Bible.

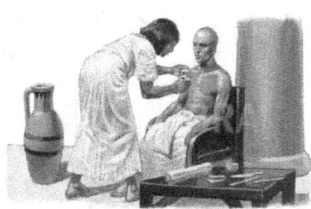

The information on this card came from ancient medical texts.

LEGENDS ABOUT HEALING WATERS -- There are places in Africa where the waters have 'healing powers' (*such as:* The Nile River... Bahir Dar, Ethiopia... Estcourt, So. Africa…and others)…that European explorers called *"The Fountain of Youth"* because of the healing powers of the waters. Some of those explorers wrote books claiming that… *"the waters gave the 'native peoples' extra long, health lives."*

IS IT A MYTH OR REALITY ?

Modern western Doctors and other healers have found that the water in certain places indeed do have "healing powers" – such as that in LOURDES, FRANCE….and others -- including some in Africa, Japan, Mexico, Germany, Sweden, etc. Studies show that those waters offer 'healing effects' because of its smaller molecular structure…which is alkaline -- and they have 'anti-oxidant' properties – all of which work to heal sick bodies.

AFRICAN VIEW OF HEALTH CARE AND ILLNESS

Archeologists have found residue of herbs and manna on mummies. Traditional Africans — from Nubians,,, to Egyptians…to Zulus…to Dogons (and others) made use of plants *(and other natural remedies such as healing waters)* — including herbs, flowers, and mushrooms — has been the method of treating ailments in all of these ancient cultures for thousands of years.

The practice of **"Oriental Medicine"** dates back thousands of years. In ancient China, the art and science of herbalism and acupuncture flourished thousands of years ago. Considered today to be the oldest book on Oriental Herbal Medicines, this book: called — ***"Seng Nong's Herbal Classic"*** ---classifies 365 species of roots, grass, woods, stones and herbal medicines.

Prior to the colonization of Jamestown in 1607, the native people of Mexico had established medical institutions that practiced traditional medicines with over 5,000 native herbal remedies. These remedies are recorded in the Badiano Codex of 1552. The *"curandero"* became the Mexican health expert who used natural treatments.

WRITE A PARAGRAPH ABOUT HOW THESE **GIFTS** HAVE/COULD HELP MODERN SOCIETY--

_____

_____

_____

_____

WRITE THE DEFINITION FOR THESE WORDS --

afro-centric = _____

ancestor = _____

ankh = _____

apartheid = _____

astrology = _____

Book of the Dead = _____

colonialism = _____

Emerald Tablet = _____

griot = _____

legacy = _____

liberation = _____

meditation = _____

papyrus = _____

IN PHOTOS: Large stone-heads found in Mexico from ancient **OLMEC** Culture.

WRITE DOWN A FEW FACTS ABOUT WHAT IS IN THESE PICTURES AND
DESCRIBE WHAT YOU LEARN FROM IT --

_____

_____

_____

_____

HOW HAVE/COULD THESE **GIFTS** HELP MODERN SOCIETY—

_____

_____

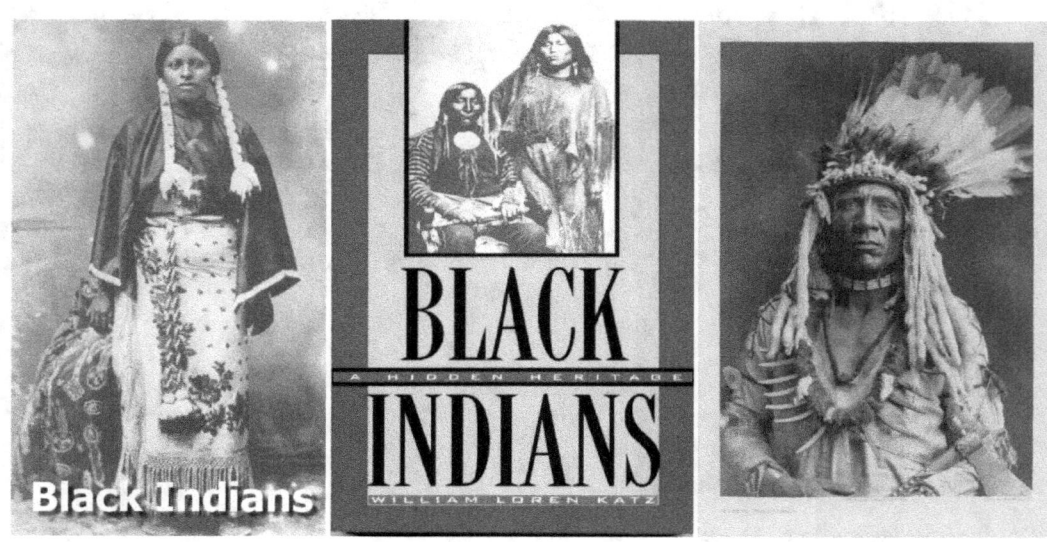

DO YOU KNOW ANYONE WHO IS CONSIDERED TO BE A 'BLACK INDIAN'?
WRITE ABOUT THEIR SITUATION ... OR ABOUT WHAT IS IN THESE PICTURES...
AND DESCRIBE WHAT YOU LEARN FROM IT --

_____

_____

_____

_____

_____

_____

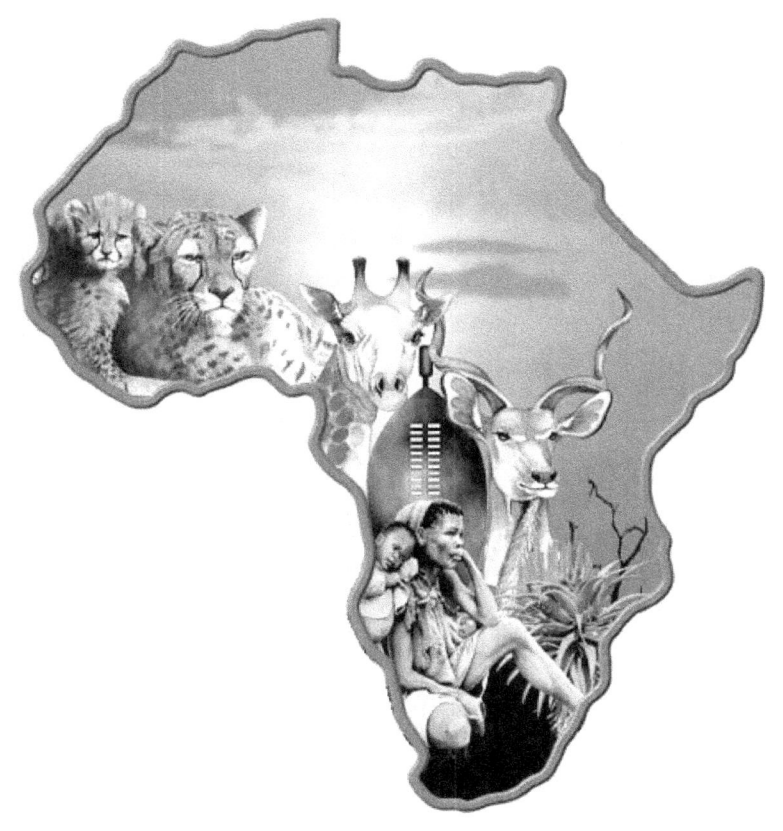

WRITE A PARAGRAPH ABOUT YOUR **FEELINGS** ABOUT OUR AFRICAN ANCESTORS

_____

_____

_____

_____

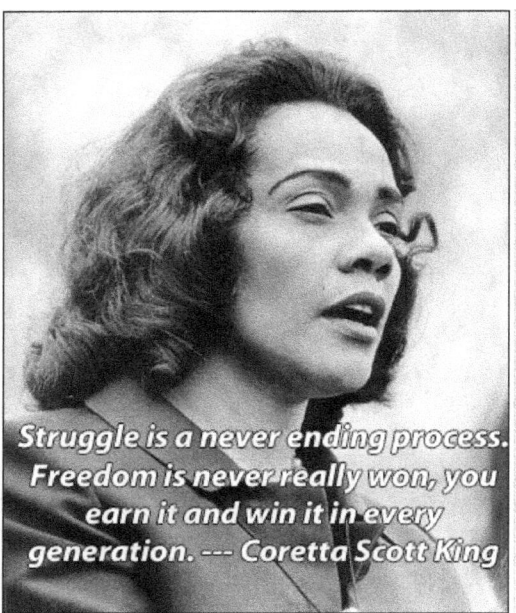

Struggle is a never ending process. Freedom is never really won, you earn it and win it in every generation. --- Coretta Scott King

If there is no struggle, there is no progress.
-Frederick Douglass

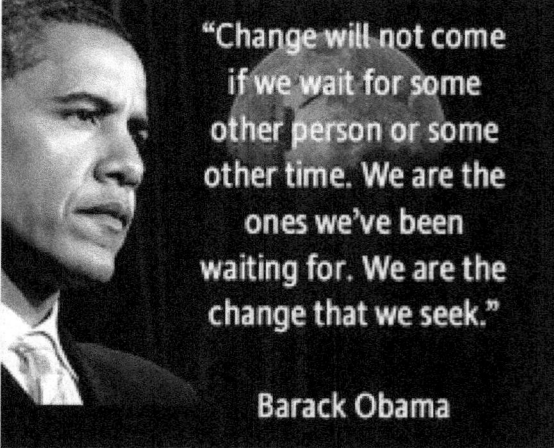

LIFE ISN'T ABOUT FINDING YOURSELF. LIFE IS ABOUT CREATING YOURSELF.

"Change will not come if we wait for some other person or some other time. We are the ones we've been waiting for. We are the change that we seek."

Barack Obama

Part Two

Secrets from our ROOTS

JET

WHAT TO EXPECT FROM FIRST BLACK MAYOR OF DETROIT

COLEMAN YOUNG

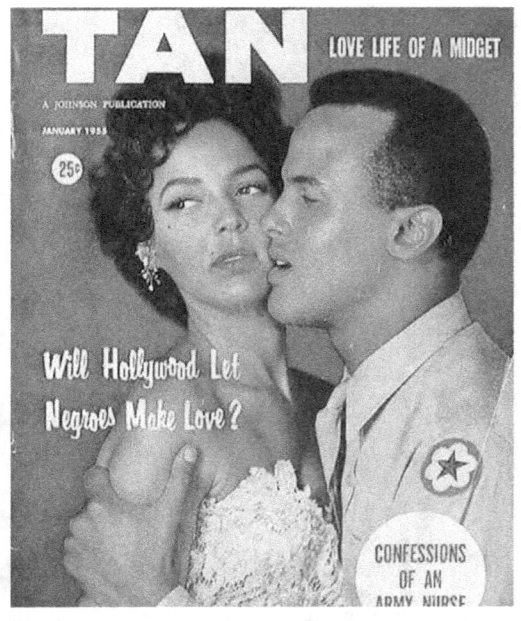

TAN

LOVE LIFE OF A MIDGET

A JOHNSON PUBLICATION

JANUARY 1955

25¢

Will Hollywood Let Negroes Make Love?

CONFESSIONS OF AN ARMY NURSE

A JOHNSON PUBLICATION

EBONY

Winston E. Moore:
MY CURE FOR PRISON RIOTS
Black penologist tells how to avoid future Atticas

THE SOUL OF CHRISTMAS
A Children's Story

ARETHA
A close-up look at Sister Superstar

DECEMBER 1971 75¢

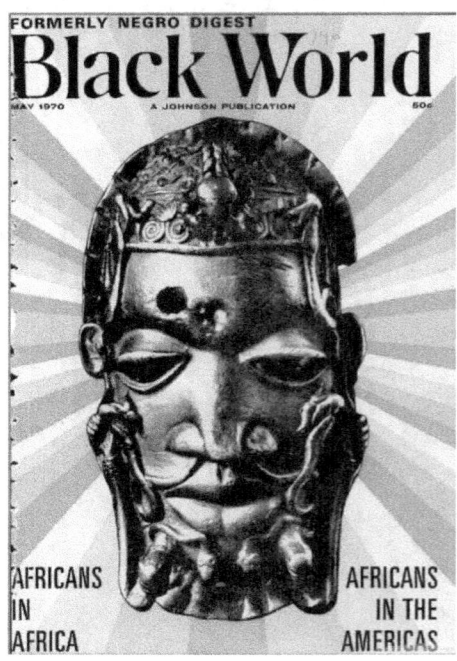

FORMERLY NEGRO DIGEST

Black World

MAY 1970   A JOHNSON PUBLICATION   50¢

AFRICANS IN AFRICA

AFRICANS IN THE AMERICAS

GOLDEN LEGACY JOURNAL

INSTRUCTIONS – Write a short description about each of the following people in the pictures….

EXAMPLES:

Mary Church Terrell
Born: September 23, 1863, Memphis, Tennessee.
Died: July 24, 1954, Annapolis, Maryland.

MARY CHURCH TERRELL WAS VERY ACTIVE
IN PUSHING FOR WOMEN'S RIGHTS AND IN FORMING
ORGANIZATIONS FOR THE BENEFIT OF WOMEN.

BIKO AND SOLIDARITY

BLACK PEOPLE'S CONVENTION
TRIBUTE TO THE LATE
HONORARY PRESIDENT
BANTU STEPHEN BIKO

1946 – 1977 Activist
against So. African
Apartheid. Killed by
police. Organizer

INCLUDE: dates, education, quotes, inventions, specialties, books, accomplishments, community service, etc.

YOU CAN ALSO CREATE YOUR OWN SCRAPBOOK OR POSTERS USING THIS INFORMATION.

Harriet Tubman

Abolitionist and Organizer
of the Underground Railroad

(c. 1822-March 10, 1913)

I freed a thousand slaves I could
have freed a thousand more if
only they knew they were
slaves. ---Harriet Tubman

**WRITE DOWN A FEW FACTS ABOUT THE PERSON IN THESE
PICTURES AND DESCRIBE WHAT YOU LEARN FROM HIM/HER --**

_____

_____

_____

HOW HAVE/COULD THESE **GIFTS** HELP MODERN SOCIETY--

_____

_____

Garrett Augustus Morgan

WRITE DOWN A FEW FACTS ABOUT THE PERSON IN THIS PICTURE AND DESCRIBE WHAT YOU LEARN FROM HIM/HER –

_____

_____

_____

HOW HAVE/COULD THESE **GIFTS** HELP MODERN SOCIETY--

_____

_____

WRITE DOWN A FEW FACTS ABOUT THE PERSON IN THIS
PICTURE AND DESCRIBE SOMETHING IMPORTANT THAT THEY
DID FOR THE IMPROVEMENT OF SOCIETY --

_____

_____

_____

_____

_____

WRITE DOWN A FEW FACTS ABOUT THE PERSON IN THESE PICTURES AND DESCRIBE WHAT YOU LEARN FROM HIM/HER –

_____

_____

_____

HOW HAVE/COULD THESE **GIFTS** HELP MODERN SOCIETY--

_____

_____

Mary McLeod Bethune
Educator for Blacks

THE BLACK AMERICAN EXPERIENCE
MARY MCLEOD BETHUNE

CHAMPION FOR EDUCATION

Follow her illustrious path from the cotton fields of the South to renowned African American educator, leader of women & champion of racial equality

African Americans who Left Their Stamp on History

WRITE DOWN A FEW FACTS ABOUT THE PERSON IN THESE PICTURES AND DESCRIBE WHAT YOU LEARN FROM HIM/HER—

_____

_____

_____

_____

HOW HAVE/COULD THESE **GIFTS** HELP MODERN SOCIETY--

_____

_____

INVENTOR

ELIJAH McCOY

McCoy's driving ambition was to find a way to oil machines as they worked

Elijah McCoy
who developed a device that oiled engines
on trains. So successful was his invention,
that for decades afterwards, consumers
would insist on purchasing
"the Real McCoy"

WRITE DOWN A FEW FACTS ABOUT THE PERSON IN THIS PICTURE AND DESCRIBE WHAT YOU LEARN FROM HIM/HER --

_____

_____

_____

HOW HAVE/COULD THESE **GIFTS** HELP MODERN SOCIETY--

_____

_____

Madame C.J. Walker
(1869 – 1919)
Cosmetics Manufacturer

I got my start by giving myself a start.
---Madam C.J. Walker

WRITE DOWN A FEW FACTS ABOUT THE PERSON IN THESE PICTURES AND DESCRIBE WHAT YOU LEARN FROM HIM/HER –

_____

_____

_____

_____

HOW HAVE/COULD THESE **GIFTS** HELP MODERN SOCIETY--

_____

_____

WRITE DOWN A FEW FACTS ABOUT THE PERSON IN THESE
PICTURES AND DESCRIBE WHAT YOU LEARN FROM HIM/HER -

_____

_____

_____

HOW HAVE/COULD THESE **GIFTS** HELP MODERN SOCIETY--

_____

_____

  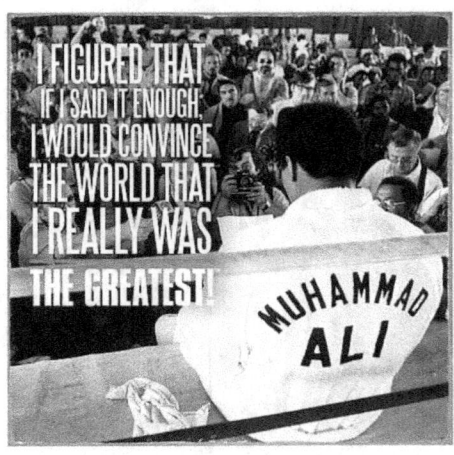

Muhammad Ali — 3 times world heavy-weight boxing champ.

WRITE DOWN A FEW FACTS ABOUT THE PERSON IN THESE
PICTURES AND DESCRIBE WHAT YOU LEARN FROM HIM/HER –

_____

_____

_____

_____

HOW HAVE/COULD THESE **GIFTS** HELP MODERN SOCIETY--

_____

_____

Dave Duerson -- NFL – Chicago Bears

David R. Duerson (born November 28, 1960 in <u>Muncie, Indiana</u>) is a former <u>American football</u> **safety** in the <u>National Football League</u> who played for the <u>Chicago Bears</u> (1983–1989), the <u>New York Giants</u> (1990), and the <u>Phoenix Cardinals</u> (1991–1993).

WRITE DOWN A FEW FACTS ABOUT THE PERSON IN THESE
PICTURES AND DESCRIBE WHAT YOU LEARN FROM HIM/HER -

_____

_____

_____

_____

_____

Fannie Lou Hamer was a dedicated freedom fighter.

WRITE DOWN A FEW FACTS ABOUT THE PERSON IN THESE PICTURES AND DESCRIBE WHAT YOU LEARN FROM HIM/HER --

_____

_____

_____

_____

HOW HAVE/COULD THESE **GIFTS** HELP MODERN SOCIETY--

_____

_____

Part Three

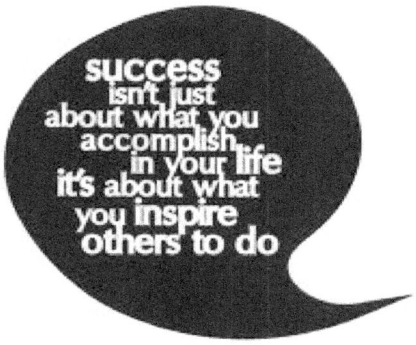

ACTIVITY: *Explore Success*

INSTRUCTIONS: Select 3 of the famous leaders, inventors, scholars, or heroes of these below – or choose 2 …plus someone else whom you admire …and perhaps would like to have a similar occupation or are great role models.

 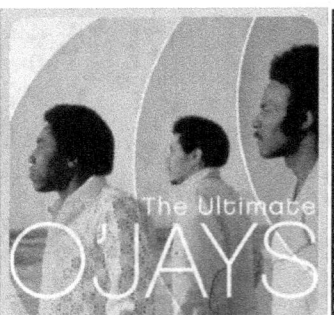  

Then answer the following questions about that person...

- What great idea did this person have that led to a great achievement?
- What type of training or education did this person use in their career?
  - How did this person contribute to the improvement of society?

Young People Who Have Made Their Mark in the World

Young man creates popular comic strip: **'BOONDOCKS'**

  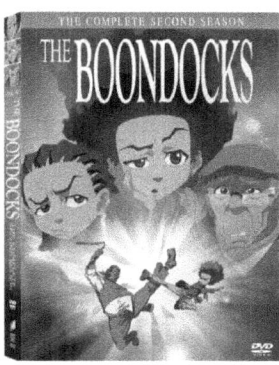

Before **Aaron Macgruder** was 30 years old, he had created and published a very popular syndicated comic strip, which debuted in 1999. Some of the episodes are now presented on DVDs and YOUTUBE.

WRITE DOWN A FEW FACTS ABOUT THE PERSON IN THESE PICTURES AND DESCRIBE ANY MESSAGES OR MORAL LESSONS IN THE "BOONDOCKS" STORIES –

_____

_____

HOW HAVE/COULD THESE **GIFTS** HELP MODERN SOCIETY--

_____

_____

WRITE THE ANSWERS TO THE QUESTIONS ABOUT THE PEOPLE YOU
HAVE SELECTED—

Person #1 _____

_____

_____

Person #2 _____

_____

_____

Person #3 _____

_____

_____

FIND A PICTURE OF YOUR FAVORITE HERO OR ROLE MODEL AND PASTE IT HERE:

Then answer the same questions about the **person you have selected**.

Person #4 _____

_____

_____

ADD A QUOTE FROM YOUR CHOSEN ROLE MODEL---

_____

_____

_____

ADD A QUOTE FROM A FAMOUS PERSON, such as:

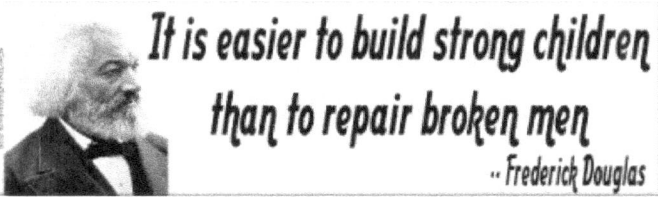

INTERVIEW ONE OF YOUR FAVORITE LEADERS

Pretend that you are a reporter who is interviewing one of your favorite leaders from past history. Write it up as you would an interview for a magazine or newspaper....including the QUESTIONS and ANSWERS....

Example --
PERSON BEING INTERVIEWED: <u>Harriet Tubman</u>

Reporter: What motivated you to want to help other slaves to escape?

Ms. Tubman: I had been a slave myself and I realized that it was an awful way to live. I believe that no human being should have to be treated so badly. Fortunately I have never had to use my gun.

Reporter: Let's talk about your child life, Harriet....when and where did you live when you were a slave?

Ms. Tubman: I was born in 1822. I lived on the Broda Plantation in Maryland. My master beat me often and I finally escaped in 1849. I went back later and helped my family to escape. Since I was a slave, my childhood was very sad and lonely as well as a lot of work. My family worked in the fields while I worked in the house.

****

WRITE A LETTER TO ONE OF YOUR FAVORITE LEADERS

A) **Compose a letter to one of your favorite leaders**, scholars, inventors or heroes of Black History.
B) Write about significant accomplishments and thank this person.

    (1) Make a list of at least 5 things that this person did to help others.
    (2) Pretend that this person is scheduled to speak at your school – and include the INTRODUCTION that you plan to give for them before the audience.
    (3) Explain how this person's invention or achievement continues to effect or influence the modern world.

USE THE FOLLOWING FILL-IN-LETTER **or** SIMPLY COMPOSE AND WRITE YOUR OWN LETTER.

YOUR LETTER...

Dear _____ ;

   I am writing to you to tell you how much I admire you for what you did back in

                           _____

...when you _____

   Because you are scheduled to be a Guest Speaker at our school in the auditorium before all the students, I am also sending you the INTRODUCTION that I plan to use when you come to the stage. The following is what I plan to say about you --

Ladies and gentleman, I am here today to introduce you to a dynamic person who...

_____

_____

_____

Whether you realize it or not – your *(invention, discovery, activities, book, etc.)* has been of great benefit for many years and we highly respect what you did because....

_____

_____

   Thank you very much for your time and interest...

Best regards.....

Signed: _____

Proverbs from Africa

* Don't insult the crocodile until you cross the water. *(Ashanti)*

* Greed led the monkey to fall on its back.

"Only a fool tests the water with both feet."

African Proverb

* The Earth is round, everything revolves…
       Give good --get good.
       Lies will grow and grow…and may
       Return to bite you.
       You reap what you sow. *(Swahili)*

* Rats don't dance in the cat's doorway.

* A little rain each day will fill the rivers to overflowing.

" Smooth seas do not make skillful sailors. "

African Proverb

HOW MUCH DO YOU KNOW ABOUT **MUSIC** ?

  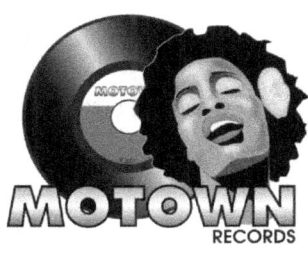

Write a short description (giving dates, style of music, what they were most famous for, and achievements) **of each musician named –**

a) Nat King Cole = _____

b) Harry Belafonte = _____

c) Nina Simone = _____

d) Big Mama Thornton = _____

e) John Coltrane = _____

The light always shows on the outside if you are striving to be good inside.
--- Erykah Badu

Faith is the black person's federal reserve system. --- Hattie McDaniel

"I have a dream that my four little children will one day live in a nation where they will not be judged by the color of their skin but by the content of their character."

Kalimbas have played a part in African culture for 800 years. After work in the evening, Africans sit in a circle, tell beautiful stories, sing and play kalimba. They are also used to pass the time on long journeys on foot.

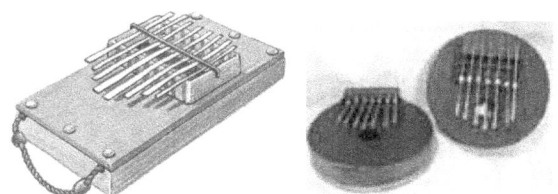

The **Kalimba** (*also called:* mbira, likembe or thumb piano) is a plucked idiophone unique to Africa and widely distributed throughout the continent. It is commonly played as an accompaniment to song, but in some areas it is used for purely instrumental music.

CHOOSE AN INSTRUMENT AND MAKE YOUR OWN –

www.activityvillage.co.uk/african_drum.htm   www.makingfriends.com/musical_instruments.htm

"Until lions have their historians, tales of the hunt shall always glorify the hunters." ~African Proverb

BACK TO THE FUTURE

Learn via *"Ol' School Music"* –

Young people refer to the music of the past – such as: ***"Motown Sounds"*** – as *"Ol School."* But perhaps if we examine the lyrics and poetry of those days – we can find messages and wisdom to help us to deal with our serious modern ailments.

OBJECTIVE OF THIS EXERCISE -- To help participants (students) to recognize the golden legacy of healthy, inspiring, and empowering messages put out by **African-American musicians and writers**...*(which could help us all to solve a lot of our modern-day problems).

INSTRUCTIONS: 1) Make a list of some of the famous musicians and their songs. *For example:*

*The Marvelettes... * Billie Holliday... * The Intruders... * The Coasters...
... * The Delfonics ...* Aretha Franklin ....* Marvin Gaye ... * Gil Scott Heron....

Many of these musicians' works can be found on old albums and/or YOUTUBE. Then write down a few lines of their **lyrics** or **poems** that offer inspiration, solutions, wise, and healthy values. Find songs (ol' school music & recordings) in which many of the musicians, writers, and artists from our past sang POSITIVE MESSAGES... about positive ways of living.

PREPARE AN EXHIBIT, DEMONSTRATION, or DRAMA to show the class or group **2 of the best ones** – (positive, educational, empowering) - with lyrics that you found....and the wisdom or remedies offered in the songs. Each student can play the songs – or small groups can ROLE PLAY the musicians performing --- and have the class sing along with them.

WISE TEACHERS MAKE LEARNING ENJOYABLE...

LESSONS FROM THE WISE: The ever-popular musical group: *"Earth, Wind & Fire"* based their music on many ancient spiritual messages, concepts, beliefs and practices.

Many other musicians educated us about liberation, ecology, spirituality, and cultures.

Part Four

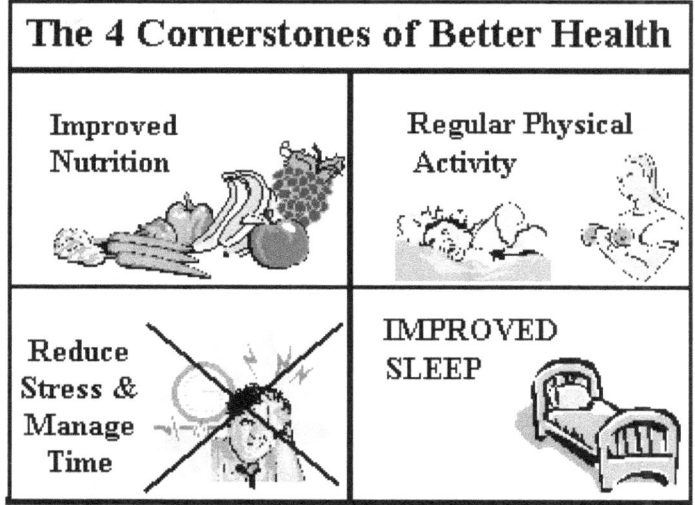

The 4 Cornerstones of Better Health

Improved Nutrition	Regular Physical Activity
Reduce Stress & Manage Time	IMPROVED SLEEP

GOOD HEALTH IS WEALTH !

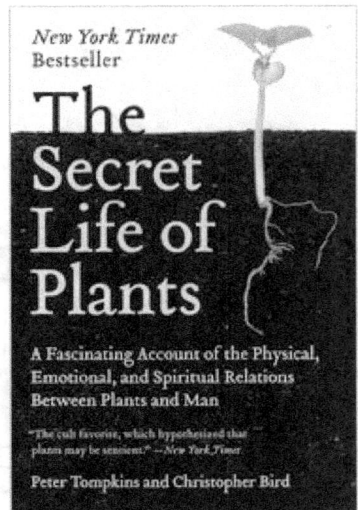

NATURE OFFERS MANY BENEFITS THAT CAN SOLVE OUR PROBLEMS

Until you discover the purpose of your life, you will live a life of mediocrity.
Rise and be great, do the great things you were meant to do. Explore
yourself, discover your purpose of life and live your passion.

ANCIENT AFRICAN HEALING METHODS

Many of the health care treatments and methods that we now call *"Holistic"* or " alternative natural remedies" – such as: Herbalism, Reiki, Reflexology, Massage, Chiropractic, Psycho-therapy, etc. -- began long ago in Africa.

HOLISTIC HEALTH and HERBALISM practices are some of the oldest techniques used for health care and they are claimed to predate all organized religions. The ancient *'medicine men'* of Kemet (Egypt) used many forms of herbal medicines, treatments, and even surgery long ago. The Ancient Africans had spiritual and philosophical systems that were very advanced. Ancient practices of Yoga, Meditation, Martial Arts, and Herbalism held incredible power to heal and de-stress. The systems that were in use are still more intellectual than most modern religions of today.

The San or Bushmen ancestors who were primarily scattered in Southern Africa before the 19th century, are reported to have practiced something similar to Shamanism. The Shaman traverses the axis mundi or world tree and enters the spirit world by effecting a transition of consciousness. This activity is done by entering into an ecstatic trance or altered state of perception; either auto-hypnotically or through the use of plants.

The methods employed are diverse, and are often used together. Some of the methods for effecting such trance states include -- *drumming, dancing, singing, fasting, chanting, sweat lodge, vision quests, etc.*

MAKE A LIST OF SICKNESSES AND THE NATURAL, HERBAL and/or HOLISTIC REMEDY FOR IT....
Examples:

Anti-virus herbs = **Goldenseal, Echinacea, Elderberry, Ginger Root, Eucalytus**

Anti-virus & bacteria foods = **onions and garlic, fruits** (Vitamin C)

Herbs for high blood pressure = **Sage, Red Yeast Rice, Hawthorne**

Foods that fight cancer and tumors = **broccoli, carrots**

WRITE IN THE NUTRITIONAL BENEFITS FOR THESE FOODS

Example: **CORN** = helps fight disease; great source of BRAIN NOURISHMENT: Thiamine, Potassium & B-vitamins

apple = _____

honey =_____

watermelon= _____

oatmeal = _____

yogurt = _____

The physician's tomb at Ankmahor, Saqqara in Ancient Egypt around 2350 BC, depicting a Reflexology treatment

WRITE DOWN A FEW FACTS ABOUT WHAT IS IN THIS PICTURE AND DESCRIBE WHAT YOU LEARN FROM IT --

_____

_____

_____

_____

_____

_____

MAKE CARDS FOR HEALTH

Select a famous leader, inventor, scholar, or hero – who has been a leader, nurse, doctor, herbalist, teacher, minister, writer, and role model in the HEALTH CARE field.

FIND A PICTURE OF YOUR FAVORITE HERO OR ROLE MODEL – AND THEIR REMEDIES -- AND PASTE IT ON A LARGE CARD...

Example: Daniel Hale Williams

MAKE A CARD ABOUT THIS LEADER...or make several about all of your choices. WHAT HEALTH REMEDIES DID THIS PERSON OFFER? You can use these for taking care of your own health – helping others – or for class presentations: **during -- *'Black History Month'... 'Earth Day'*** (etc.)

- What great idea did this person have that led to an important achievement?
- What type of experiences, training did this person use to enter into their career?
- How did this person contribute to the improvement of society?
- Add an inspirational QUOTE made by this person.

Example --

MAKE YOUR OWN HEALTH REMEDY CARD FILE –

Prepare cards by putting the name of a sickness, ailment, or other health problem on each one. Then match each with – a

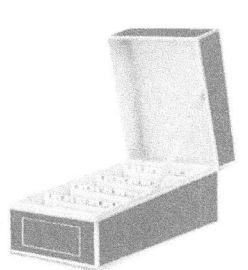

suggested good, harmless remedies for each.

Keep your cards in a file box in alphabetical order – so that it is easy to access the information when you want it.

HEALTH FOOD STORES HAVE LOTS OF GOOD INFO THAT YOU CAN USE...

MAKE HEALTHY CHOICES

Circle the images showing the healthiest choices.

Draw a circle around the most HEALTHY activities.

Then, draw your own picture of a way to stay healthy...including good foods to eat. Add a short paragraph explaining your picture.

The U.S.D.A. recommends that more than half our meals contain vegetables and fruits.

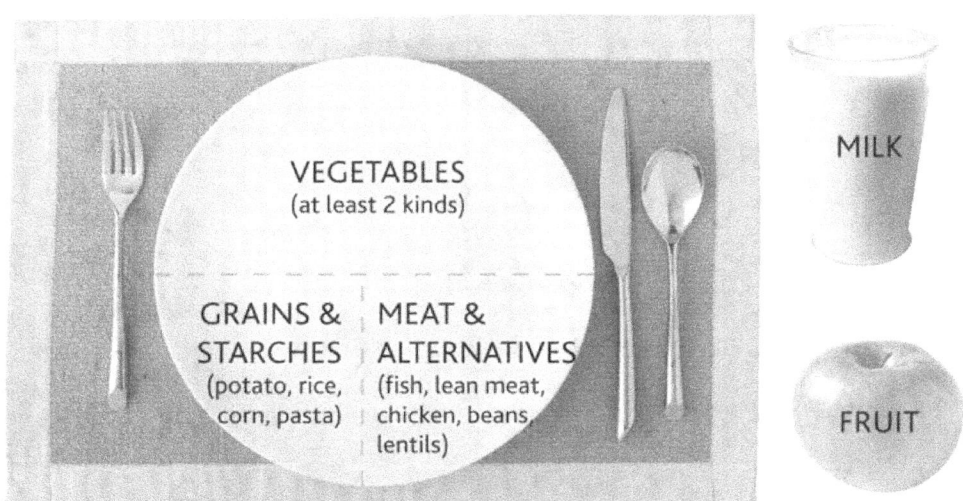

WRITE A **MEAL HEALTHY PLAN** FOR YOUR NEXT DINNER --

_____

_____

Vegetables_____

Grains _____

Fruit _____

Beverage _____

Comments: _____

Drug addict

CIGARETTES AND DRUGS CAUSE CANCER AND OTHER DISEASES

What cigarettes are made of ---

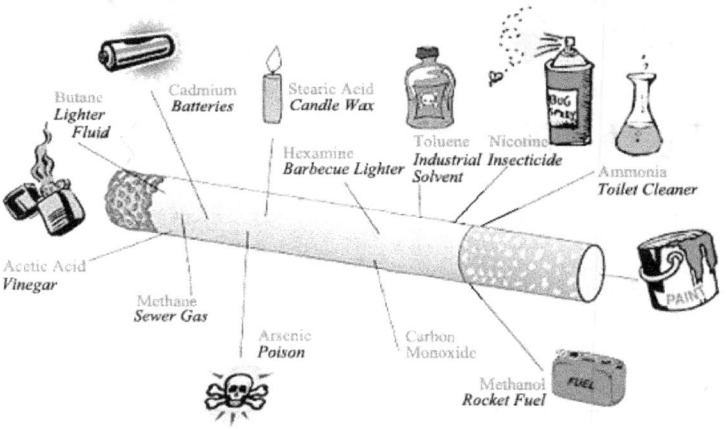

WRITE A SHORT PARAGRAPH ABOUT WHY PEOPLE SHOULD
SAY NO TO DRUGS, ALCOHOL, AND CIGARETTES ---

_____

_____

_____

ARE THERE ANSWERS TO THE SERIOUS PROBLEMS?
IS THERE A GURU OR ADVANCED MASTER TEACHER WHO CAN HELP US?

Yes, there are remedies! Many of the answers to our most pressing problems and difficult challenges are right before our eyes.

EXERCISE -- Write a short paragraph about the philosophy, ideas, and achievements of each of the following --

a) Majora Carter

b) Rachel Carson

c) James Lovelock

d) John Muir

e) Wangari Maathai

f) Ted Turner

g) Van Jones

All of these people listed above had something in common. They believed we should...

ACTIVITY: SELECT ONE OF THESE PEOPLE and make a poster (or other artistic creation) about their contributions.

Wangari Maathai
Green Belt Movement of Kenya

Each of the ancient ethnic groups (or "tribes") of Africa has its own distinct language, culture, and religion, etc. But they did have one common value – which was a reverence for – the Earth and environment. They assigned high status to the sun, moon, stars, plants and animals – in a *holistic* way. They saw all these elements as *"sacred"* …and not just as objects. The ancient **Kemet**ic people's view of religion (spirituality) came from studying aspects of Nature, which viewed systematically, represents "God" anywhere. Because of the African's reverence for Nature – many White Western explorers and writers **mis-interpreted** that as a form of *'paganism.'*

BASED UPON THE ANCIENT AFRICAN PERSPECTIVE ON ENVIRONMENT, WRITE A FEW WORDS EXPLAINING HOW THE ANCIENTS MIGHT VIEW WHAT MODERN MAN HAS DONE TO THE EARTH --

_____

_____

_____

_____

_____

_____

MAKE A POSTER OR COLLAGE

Select any **topic** from this workbook and use it to create your own educational lesson or important message. Cut out pictures from old magazines, newspapers, photocopy some, and print out some clip-art or illustrations from websites.... *Paste them on to a large poster board.

Then -- add your own info, messages and/or *'words of wisdom'* to your poster.

Invention/ achievement .... BLACK Contributor/ Inventors

Air conditioner ---------------------------- Frederick Jones

Blood & plasma system ------------------ Dr. Charles Drew..(1940)

Clock (1st American) ------------------ Benjamin Banneker

Electric clothes dryer -------------------------- George T. Samon

Electric devices for trains -------------------- Granville T. Woods

Elevator ------------------------------- Alexander Miles

Hair dressing & straightening --------- Madame C. J. Walker.... (1905)

Light bulb ...and electric lamp -------------- Louis Latimer... (1886)

Printing Press ------------------------------ W. A. Lavalette

Refrigerator -------------------------------- John Standard

Shoe stitching machine ----------------- Jan Matzeliger ...(1883)

Traffic signal & gas mask ------------------ Garrett Morgan

www.african-americaninventors.org   www.blackinventor.com

During the *"Occupy Wall Street"* protests – the critics and opponents of this movement offered off-base arguments.... That...*"the economic problems were caused by President Obama's policies"* – and some critics said... " the 99%-ers...the marchers and those angry at Wall Street **were actually "anti-capitalism."** Those critics claimed that ...*"free market capitalism"* is the reason we have so many wonderful inventions, good technology, indoor plumbing, cell phones, a rich nation, etc.

ACTIVITY: Select 2 or 3 Black inventors and then MAKE A POSTER... a collage – using pictures of the inventors and their creations... and words. Your poster should show reasons why and how so many BLACK PEOPLE have created such fantastic inventions, but yet – *unemployment, poverty, sickness, and suffering* have been so widespread and much worse for Black people than for any other group.

Chief Joseph ~ Nez Perce

The earth is the mother of all people, and all people should have equal rights upon it

The natural world is the larger sacred community to which we belong. —Thomas Berry

MAKE YOUR OWN ALPHABET BOOK

SUPPLIES NEEDED: Sheets of paper, glue stick, old magazines.

Using regular typing paper, fold sheets in half to make pages for your book.

 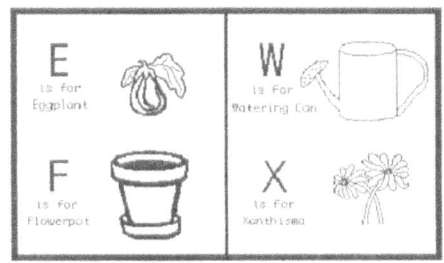

CHOOSE A TITLE AND THEME FOR YOUR BOOK

YOUR BOOK CAN BE ABOUT NATURE, HEALTH, ECOLOGY, GLOBAL WARMING ...OR BIOS ABOUT SCIENTISTS & SCHOLARS WHO HAVE CONTRIBUTED TOWARD IMPROVING MEDICINES...OR ANY SIMILAR TOPIC.

Lay the pages out so that the pictures will be in alphabetical order when it is finished and the spine is stapled.

Begin your book with the LETTER A.

Find pictures or illustrations of foods or other natural items that begin with "A" and paste them in that section.

EXAMPLES: **A is for Africa**
B = Black History
C = culture

D = _____

You can be as *creative* as you wish in making the contents of your booklet.

The finished book will be **5.5" x 8"** after putting all folded sheets together.

If you wish, make the outside cover out of cardstock. Place **STAPLES**

down the spine of the book (fold) to finish it.

Example --

Celebrating Black History Month

Our journal

Name _____

Name of Person _____

Name of Person _____

GROUP ACTIVITIES

"Substitute for Health" GAME

GOAL = To learn how to select, prepare and eat better foods.

LEVEL = ages 14 to adult

HOW TO START – Find a friend or partner who will do it with you. Each of you will write a list of all the foods and drinks that you consumed for the past 3 days.

FOR EXAMPLE:

Monday --- **BREAKFAST** = eggs, toast, cheese, cereal, milk
LUNCH --- Burger King = cheese burger, fries and coke
DINNER --- 4 pcs. fried chicken, mashed potatoes, roll and 3 pcs. cake.
SNACKS = 2 diet cokes and 1 bag potato chips.

After completing your list, **TRADE it** with your partner.

Each participant will review the other person's list --- and then make suggestions as to how to improve the diet--- additions, substitutes, etc.

EXAMPLE: Stop drinking so much coke and drink APPLE JUICE…instead. Eat a banana or apple for breakfast. Add a salad for dinner.

When both parties are finished writing their SUGGESTIONS, meet together to discuss the plans for HEALTHIER EATING.

AFTER **ONE SESSION**--- find 2 more people to participate and do the activity again. This time, there will be 4 people trading lists. Continue until you build a circle of "healthy eaters." You can then have **"get togethers"** or **dinner parties** – cook and eat HEALTHY FOODS together occasionally.

** If you wish – find **nutrition reference books or websites** to help decide on healthier foods.

EDUTAINMENT GAMES --- DESIGN STAMPS
A FUN GROUP LEARNING ACTIVITY

INSTRUCTIONS -- The **U.S. Post Office** published many stamps which honored various heroes, holidays, inventors, athletes, good causes, and Black Achievers. **CHOSE A TOPIC** or GOOD CAUSE... and find as many STAMPS as you can via the Internet, old magazines (etc.) – and perhaps some you may have at home (which you can photocopy). Select a leader, scholar, athlete, scientist, writer, actor, politician, musician, or other achiever --- then **make your own stamp** for that person. Paste up at least 6 of these stamps onto a large cardboard with your own creation -- and create a presentation for ***BLACK HISTORY MONTH or EARTH DAY...*** (or another event) at your school.

Work with 2 - 4 other people to make card games. You can also paste your stamps onto 3" X 5" cards and make card games out of them – such as, **'CONCENTRATION'** -- or the old popular one -- **'GO FISH.'**

KEEP CARDS AND HAVE MANY HOURS OF FUN – PLAYING GAMES AND LEARNING.

CREATE GAMES FROM STAMPS

Adapt the cards that you make from the Black History or your chosen THEMED Stamps to these popular fun card games. For example -- themes such as: "BLACK MUSICIANS" ....or ... "GREEN ENERGY."

' GO FISH '

Instructions -- Make 2 matching cards for each stamp by pasting the stamp on one side of a blank 3" x 5" card. You will need a deck of at least 40 cards. Once the deck is complete, a group of 3 to 6 people can play the game. Play the card game similar to the old popular one known as "GO FISH."

Each player gets 6 cards from the dealer – to begin the game. The object is to find the match for each card. Players take turns – first by asking the player on their right for one card. EXAMPLE: *"Do you have a **Rosa Parks** stamp?"*

If the player on the right has that card – he/she must give it to the player who asked for it. The player then lays the matches out in front of his place...and continues. If not – the player will respond ... **"Go Fish !"** The first player must then draw 2 cards from the deck. Then, the next player has a turn to do the same thing.

This game continues around the circle until someone gets the matches to all of their cards.

' CONCENTRATION '

Instructions -- Using the same deck of cards – students can play the game known as: *"Concentration."* In this game ... distribute the cards – **face down** – in several rows. Players will take turns --- the first player will turn over a card. Then the player must select any other card and turn it over. If it matches – the player keeps both matching cards...and gets another turn to find 2 more matching cards. If it does not match – then the player turns both cards back down as they were. The players continue taking turns...until all the matches have been found. Whoever has the most cards will be the winner.

Note: *Teachers can offer prizes for game winners.*

ROCK SCHOOL GAME

GOALS & OBJECTIVES

To practice answering questions with facts...and to learn more about history or other topics.

MATERIALS NEEDED:

* This game is best played on a set of steps or bleachers. Each step is considered to be a "grade level"--- e.g. *"First grade, second grade, third grade, etc."* The top step is GRADUATION.

* Prepare a list of at least 100 questions with their answers---on the facts and events of Black History – or any subject that you choose.

EXAMPLE:
*Q = What is the name of the famous Black Basketball team that began in 1927 and won more than 8,000 games?

* *Answer =* **The Harlem Globetrotters.**

HOW TO PLAY THIS GAME:

The group leader or teacher hides a small stone or rock in one hand, with both hands behind his/her back....as s/he faces the players who are sitting on the steps. Each player will take a turn to guess which hand the teacher is hiding the stone. If the player guesses correctly, then the teacher gives this same player one of the QUESTIONS to answer. If the player answers correctly, s/he gets to move up one step. Then the next player gets a turn to do the same.

Each player will have no more than one minute to give their answer to each question.

If the player does not get the right answer as to which hand the rock is in...the player loses his/her turn. If the player does not get the correct answer to the question, the player has gets demoted one step (and must move down one step).

THE WINNER is the player who reaches the top step first.

* Prizes can be awarded to the players who reach the top grades.

INTERNET SCAVENGER HUNT

Objective: To increase research skills by using the Internet to find facts about various subjects, topics or historical events. This is an excellent exercise for teaching *Black (African-American) History*.

Supplies needed: Computers with Internet access & printer.
Paper and pens

How to Play:

Based upon a lesson or subject being taught or discussed, have the ENTIRE GROUP of students or participants prepare a list of at least 100 questions that they want to research---
FOR EXAMPLE:
* How many miles is the distance from Earth to the Sun?
* Name 3 products created by Dr. G. W. Carver from peanuts.
* What is Melanin and where is it usually found?

Participants are later divided into groups of 3 in each team.

Each team will have an equal number of the questions to research via using the Internet.

As a group, the teams will use *"Search Engines"* and websites to research and find the answers to as many questions on their list as possible. The teams must work together to find and write their answers. Answers should be less than one-half page in length (2 to 3 paragraphs at most).

After 30 min. the teams must present their QUESTIONS and ANSWERS to the entire group verbally. Answers must be logical, correct and thorough.

The team that gets the most correct and thorough answers---WINS.

SPREAD POSITIVE MESSAGES
DESIGN YOUR OWN INSPIRATIONAL T-SHIRT

ART-FUN FOR GROUPS…Make an positive shirt-message design for a poster or t-shirt

Find pictures, info, slogans, and ideas -- and then create your POSITIVE MESSAGE.
Use a **t-shirt** on which you can print your art-work and message.   Find *iron-on* **labels**
via an *Office Supply Store* or from the Internet …to create your own unique messages.
Or you can cut out **paper-shirts**, and make a poster.

www.avery.com   www.customink.com   www.labelyourstuff.com

FOR MORE FUN – SPONSOR A CONTEST… find supporters who will donate
prizes and then get more other people to join you in making their own t-shirts with
unique POSITIVE MESSAGES. And -- the group can have each designer parade
around their class, seminar, club, team, etc. -- to display what each created.
Or – help RAISE FUNDS for your group with these gifts.

You can also create: BUMPER STICKERS, BADGETS, SIGNS, BUTTONS, HATS, COASTERS, AND OTHER GIFTS...

 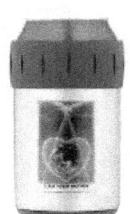 

A place to find good, inspirational messages ...

www.ecofuture.net/greenslogans   www.recyclereminders.com

www.africanamericanquotes.org

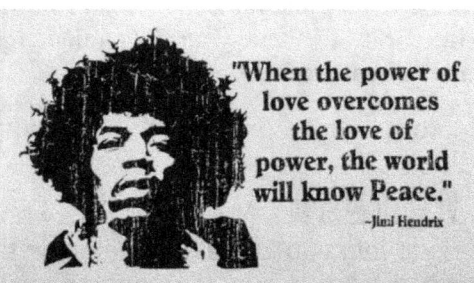 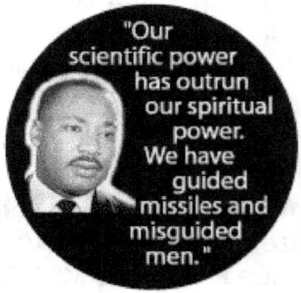

CONTACT US FOR MORE INFO ON IMPRINTED PRODUCTS -- get-paid@hotmail.com

Part Five

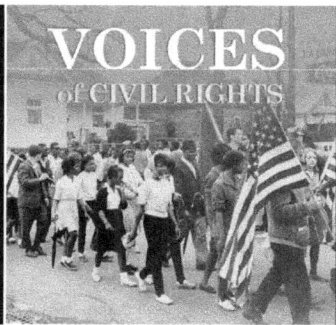

ACTION SPEAKS LOUDER THAN **WORDS**

SOMETIMES SOLUTIONS ARE NOT SIMPLE AND EASY ... AND WE MUST TAKE ACTION TO SEEK SOLUTIONS TO MAJOR PROBLEMS...

Children beg for food while half the world eats too much

WRITE A PARAGRAPH ABOUT A MAJOR SOCIAL OR POLITICAL PROBLEM THAT CONCERNS YOU …

DESCRIBE YOUR PLAN OF ACTION -- How will you address your concerns?

_____ Join a protest group   ____ Help raise funds to donate   _____Register people to vote

_____ Distribute flyers, buttons, brochures & info   ____ Help a politician campaign

_____ OTHER ACTIONS: _____

CREATE YOUR OWN PLAN OF ACTION

An action plan is a simple method of documenting the following things --

1. What needs to be done? (Goals, mission, objectives)
2. Potential remedies and solutions for the problem or crisis.
3. *Who needs to do it… (trainers, suppliers, committee, Gov't officials, etc.)*
4. When it needs to be done by….dates, time, schedule.
5. Resources & revenue needed to accomplish plan…to reach goals.
6. Budget – expenses, salaries, supplies *(increased financial impact)* etc.
7. Measurements of results -- benefits, consequences, etc.

PREPARE A CHART OR OUTLINE OF YOUR ACTIONS…

Example:

The local issue to be addressed is: *LITTER* because *there lots of it around the school*

ACTION PLAN TASK TO BE COMPLETED	WHO	WHEN	INFORMATION RESOURCES WE NEED
1. MAKE POSTERS AND HAND THEM OUT	A little group	1 day	A photo copier
2. LOTS MORE BINS WITH LIDS	Banuyk	By the end of the week	Banuyk city council
3. MORE MAD	EVERYBODY (Students)	By the end of the shool Year	More Gloves (2 each)
4. HAVE A SPECIAL DAY WHERE NO PACKAGING ALOUD	TEACHERS SEND NOTISES	1 every week	PAPER
5. TELLING PEOPLE OFF WHEN YOU SEE THEM LITTER	EVERYBODY IN THE SCHOOL	EVERY DAY	
6. VIDIEO ON WHAT WOULD HAPPEN	ME	2 WEEKS	VIDEO CAMERA RUBBISH

Your plan can be as simple or complicated as necessary.

The ultimate tragedy
is not the brutality
of the bad people
but the silence
of the good people.

Remembering
Martin Luther King, Jr.
1929-1968

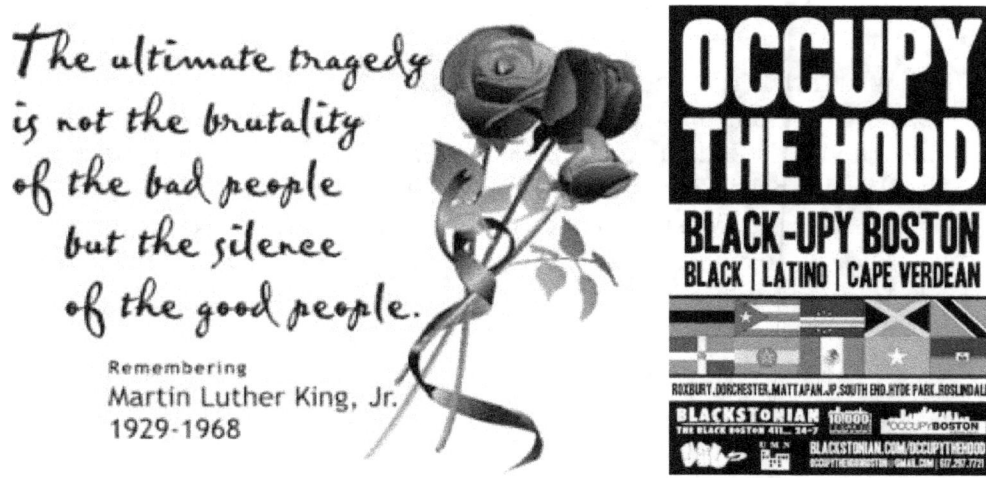

"Racism is not an excuse
to not do the best you can!"

"Do your little bit of good where you are;
it's those little bits of good put together
that overwhelm the world"

"We must be the change
we wish to see in the world."

Part Six

Learn natural ways to heal and lose weight…

FREE WEIGHT LOSS PROGRAMS: www.sparkpeople.com

www.fitday.com   www.freedieting.com

www.**letsmove**.gov

"Be the change you want to see in the world."   ~ Mahatma Ghandi

SOURCES FOR FREE STUFF

You can win great prizes

Award-winning Author M. Miller gives away free gifts, books, DVDs, CDs, and cars — to promote success and wealth and support good causes

Send $3.00 for *"Success Secrets News"*

We put the names of our customers and clients into a drawing every 3 months.

Names are drawn and gifts given away to winners.

Edutainment Enterprises

www.success-secrets.ws

Really Good Free Stuff

www.1freestuffplace.com

www.freestufftimes.com

www.freestuff.com

www.sweetfreestuff.com

www.all-free-samples.com

www.freeadvice.com

www.bestfreestuffonline.com

www.totallyfreestuff.com

www.shop4freebies.com

www.justfreestuff.com

www.freecenter.com/stuff.html

www.bargainsavingnetwork.com

www.legalforfree.com/main

www.thunderfap.com

Black History and Cultural Diversity:

www.asian-nation.org

www.awesomelibrary.org

www.buffalosoldier.net

www.thekingcenter.org

www.thewright.org

www.raceandhistory.com

www.blackhistory.com

www.black-legacy.webs.com

www.biography.com/blackhistory

www.trinity.edu/~mkearl/race.html

www.biography.com/hispanic-heritage

www.biography.com/womens-history

www.salto-youth.net/culturaldiversity

www.frenchcreoles.com/BlackIndians.html

You can win valuable prizes !

BLACK HISTORY QUIZ

QUESTIONS --

1) Who started the official Black History Month observance? Why was February selected as the month to celebrate Black History?

2) Name 2 facts about the African continent & people prior to the Trans-Atlantic Slave Trade.

3) Did the original Egyptians have help from 'aliens' (ancient astronauts) to build huge pyramids ? Evidence?

4) What is **Kwanzaa** -- and how (why) did it get started?

5) Who was Willie Lynch -- and what did he do that effected history?

6) Give a brief description of the first (original) Egyptians.

7) Name 2 of the important contributions of Dr. Carter Woodson?

8) Name 3 African-American (Black) inventors and describe their creations.

NOTE TO READERS: If you can answer some of these HISTORY questions -- in brief, but with facts, references or quotes from experts – you can earn **free** autographed books -- and other gifts.

FOR FULL DETAILS, CONTACT: culturaldiversity@hotmail.com

With books, you see the world in a whole new way.

"Falling in love with reading will open doors to the mind, heart, and soul. Reading makes life more interesting. Readers learn many fantastic things from books that they would not ordinarily know."

THE VALUE OF HISTORY   (poem by **Melvia Miller**)

People grow much like a tree...
Reaching high
Up to the sky
Yearning to breathe free!

Much like a tree
Our roots need a deep hole--
Knowing our history...
Can heal wounds and sooth souls.

A strong tree
Needs deep roots.
It is the symbol of liberty
Reaching for the light of the sun
Desiring to grow into the truth.

Without truth about our godly role...
Pain, suffering and mental anguish
Manifest from the hole made in our souls
Due to the nourishment that is missed.

All souls are on a journey
To become liberated.
Look back in history
Memory to see
From whence we were all created.

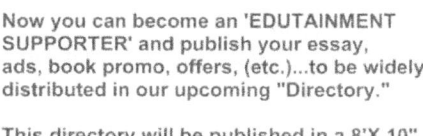

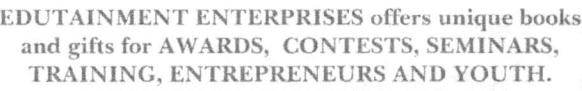

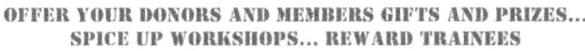

WHAT PEOPLE ARE SAYING --

" Melvia Miller is remarkable. She has the vision--the dream of racial harmony and peace on Earth. To write about this topic with laughter and love is brilliant." --

~from Ms. **Dottie Walters**, author of "SPEAK & GROW RICH"

****

"Melvia Miller brings to her work a solid background as an educator and a member of a minority group, which make her books of a true multi-cultural perspective. "   ...~from **Dr. Penny Ralston**, Dean --
Florida State Univ.

****

"I am indeed impressed with Melvia's books.
I look forward to reading more from her."

~from Dr. **Gloria Murray,** Professor--
Indiana Univ. --Louisville

"Melvia Miller writes an excellent brand of poetry." -

~by **Max Robinson**, (ABC-TV news anchorman)

"I received my copy of your book: *NEW & DIFFERENT FRIENDS*. I enjoyed reading it. So, I took it up to the nearby public library and read it to a group of young kids for their 'story time' activity. It was a lot of fun. They all loved your book so much that they wanted to keep it."

~ from **Ms. Norma Estep**, union worker retiree
(80-yrs. old)   Dayton , OH

ABOUT THE AUTHOR

Video History Museum

Would you like to visit a Black History Museum? True History Museum? Well, now you can bring one to your home.

No you can relly learn from TV. Topics includes Africa; Black History; herbs; spirituality; women; ancient sciences, and much more.

The videos are prefect for classrooms, churches, TV shows, colleges, and other educational programs.

Melvia F. Miller, is the founder and president. Her book *New and Different Friends* has been hailed and praised by teachers, parents and children as an epic symbolic story about true oneness of humanity. Many people now refer to her has "Dr. Seuss of the ghetto."

Earn while you learn from TV.

For further details and information, send a large self-addressed envelope with no less hta $1.00

EDUTAINMENT ENTERPRISES
P.O. Box 31043
Las Vegas, NV 891731-043

www.black-legacy.webs.com

Super Sistah says…

"Wake up everybody, …it's time to teach a new way."

www.success-secrets.ws